TOUGH, TOUGH TRACTORS

BENDON®
Publishing International, Inc.

© 2013
Ashland, OH 44805
www.bendonpub.com

all images © Dreamstime, iStockPhoto LP and Shutterstock, Inc.

TRACTORS

are tough.

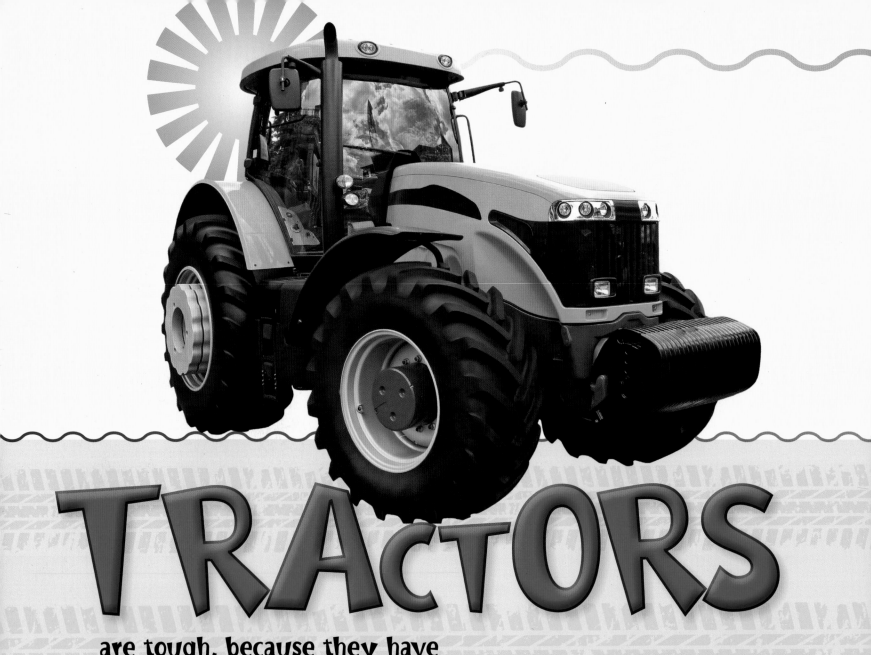

TRActORS

are tough, because they have tough jobs to do.

Farmers use them to help with CROPS.

OATS

Crops include the foods we eat-like CORN- and food grown for animals-such as hay, oats, and barley.

5

To work in farmers' fields, tractors have to have BIG TIRES.

That's because
TRACTORS
need to work in rough ground with lots of rocks.

They may also have to go up and down STEEP HILLS.

A TRACTOR'S TIRES

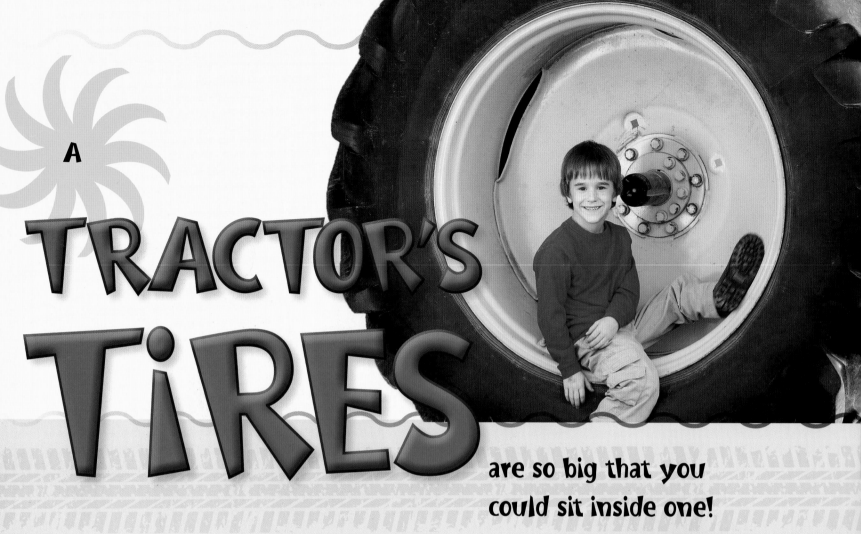

are so big that you could sit inside one!

On the outside of the tires, the tires have deep GROOVES.

GROOVES help the tire grip the dirt when the tractor goes uphill—and downhill.

One of the

BIGGEST

jobs tractors have is to

PULL.

In the spring, they pull a FURROW PLOW to break up clods of dirt.

Then they plant seeds.

When it's summer, the tractors add fertilizer to the crops to help the

PLANTS GROW.

With lots of **SUNLIGHT** and water, the plants grow tall and healthy.

In the **FALL**, it's time for the farmers to start the **HARVEST.**

The TRACTOR has special tools to cut the crop.

But the TRACTOR'S

job isn't over!

Now the TRACTOR gets to WORK again!

The FARMER uses the TRACTOR to take the crops to the market. ••••

Fresh
Garlic
*Delicious & so easy to peel!
$3.00/lb

*Super
Tender
2/lb

Cardinale
Lettuce
$2⁵⁰/ea

There you can buy the
CROPS for a fall feast!

TRACTORS

ARE GREAT!

QUESTIONS

1. How do farmers use tractors?

2. Do tractors have tiny wheels or big wheels?

3. Can a tractor pull up clods of dirt?

4. What can a tractor do in summer to help the farmer?

5. Can a tractor be used in the Fall, too? How?

6. How many tractors do you see in this book?

7. Do tractors help or hurt with farming? How?

ACTIVITIES

1 If you could have a tractor pull anything, what would it be?

_____

2 Draw your own tractor. Don't forget the big wheels!

3 What color would you paint your tractor? Use crayons to color your drawing above.

_____

4 Would you like to drive a tractor on a farm? How about drive a tractor to school every day?